SCIENCE KIDS
Life Cycles
Robins

Katie Gillespie

LET'S READ
AV²
BY WEIGL™
ADDED VALUE • AUDIO VISUAL

Go to **www.av2books.com**, and enter this book's unique code.

BOOK CODE

H739723

AV² by Weigl brings you media enhanced books that support active learning.

AV² provides enriched content that supplements and complements this book. Weigl's AV² books strive to create inspired learning and engage young minds in a total learning experience.

Your AV² Media Enhanced books come alive with...

Audio
Listen to sections of the book read aloud.

Video
Watch informative video clips.

Embedded Weblinks
Gain additional information for research.

Try This!
Complete activities and hands-on experiments.

Key Words
Study vocabulary, and complete a matching word activity.

Quizzes
Test your knowledge.

Slide Show
View images and captions, and prepare a presentation.

... and much, much more!

Published by AV² by Weigl
350 5th Avenue, 59th Floor New York, NY 10118
Website: www.av2books.com

Library of Congress Control Number: 2015958822

ISBN 978-1-4896-4507-4 (hardcover)
ISBN 978-1-4896-4508-1 (softcover)
ISBN 978-1-4896-4510-4 (multi-user eBook)

Printed in the United States of America in Brainerd, Minnesota
1 2 3 4 5 6 7 8 9 0 19 18 17 16 15

122015
041215

Project Coordinator: Jared Siemens
Art Director: Terry Paulhus

The publisher acknowledges Corbis Images, Alamy, iStock, and Getty Images as the primary image suppliers for this title.

SCIENCE KIDS
Life Cycles

Robins

CONTENTS

All animals begin life, grow, and have babies. The baby animals grow up and become parents as well. This is called a life cycle.

5

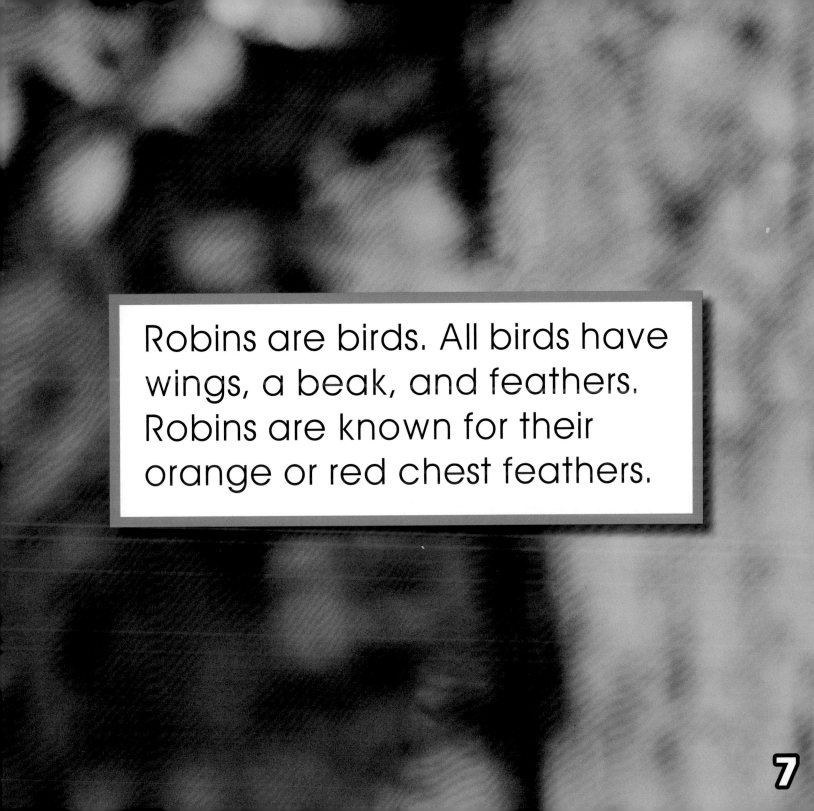

Robins are birds. All birds have wings, a beak, and feathers. Robins are known for their orange or red chest feathers.

A baby robin is born when it hatches from an egg. It uses its beak to make small holes in the shell. Then, the baby robin pushes its way out.

Robin eggs are light blue.

9

10

Baby robins are called nestlings. Only some parts of their bodies have feathers. These feathers are called down.

Nestlings can not see when they first hatch.

Robins eat and grow for about two weeks. Then, they leave the nest and learn to fly. Robins are called fledglings at this stage of the life cycle.

Robins are adults at about one year of age. They can have babies the spring after they are born. This is the adult stage of the life cycle.

16

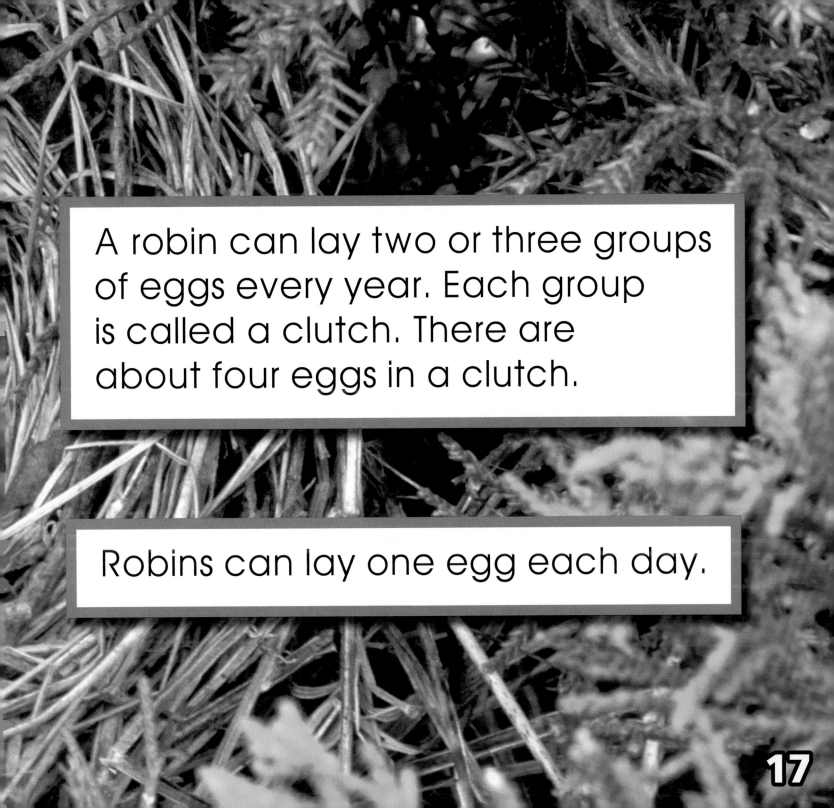

A robin can lay two or three groups of eggs every year. Each group is called a clutch. There are about four eggs in a clutch.

Robins can lay one egg each day.

A mother robin sits on her eggs for about 14 days. She does this to keep them warm.
This is called brooding.

Robins do not brood until the full clutch has been laid.

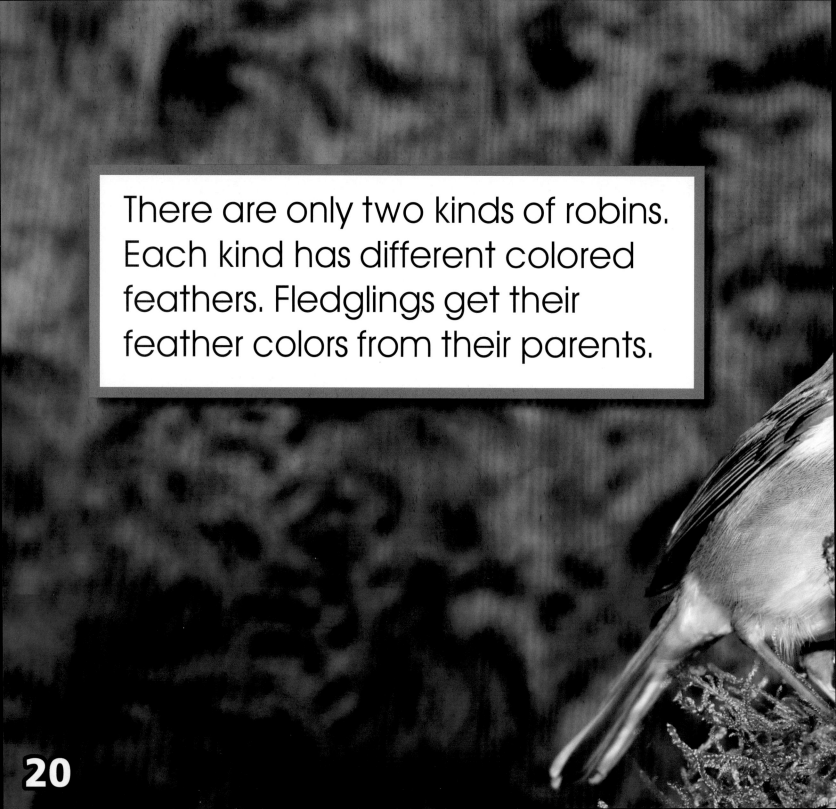

There are only two kinds of robins. Each kind has different colored feathers. Fledglings get their feather colors from their parents.

21

Life Cycles Quiz

Test your knowledge of a robin's life cycle by taking this quiz. Look at these pictures. Which stage of the life cycle do you see in each picture?

Egg   Nestling
Fledgling   Adult

KEY WORDS

Research has shown that as much as 65 percent of all written material published in English is made up of 300 words. These 300 words cannot be taught using pictures or learned by sounding them out. They must be recognized by sight. This book contains 72 common sight words to help young readers improve their reading fluency and comprehension. This book also teaches young readers several important content words, such as proper nouns. These words are paired with pictures to aid in learning and improve understanding.

Page	Sight Words First Appearance
4	a, all, and, animals, as, grow, have, is, life, the, this, up, well
7	are, for, or, their
8	an, from, in, it, its, light, make, out, small, then, to, uses, way, when
11	can, down, first, not, of, only, parts, see, some, these, they
12	about, at, eat, learn, leave, two
15	after, one, year
17	day, each, every, four, groups, there, three
19	been, do, does, has, her, keep, mother, on, she, them, until
20	different, get, kinds

Page	Content Words First Appearance
4	babies, life cycle, parents
7	beak, birds, feathers, robins, wings
8	egg, holes, shell
11	nestlings
12	fledglings, nest, stage, weeks
15	adults, spring
17	clutch
19	brooding

Check out www.av2books.com for activities, videos, audio clips, and more!

1 Go to www.av2books.com.

2 Enter book code. H739723

3 Fuel your imagination online!

www.av2books.com